# Personal Finance Activities

New York, New York    Columbus, Ohio    Chicago, Illinois

## TO THE TEACHER

**Personal Finance Activities** *provide students with the opportunity to learn valuable skills of money management. The activities in this booklet correspond to the topics found in the Personal Finance Handbook, which is located in the backmatter of your economics textbook. Each activity provides step-by-step instructions for completing the activity and gives the students the opportunity to apply what they have learned outside of the classroom.*

*Answers to the Personal Finance Activity questions can be found at the back of this booklet.*

Send all inquiries to:

Glencoe/McGraw-Hill
8787 Orion Place
Columbus, OH 43240

ISBN:    978-0-07-878058-5
MHID:    0-07-878058-6

Printed in the United States of America

5 6 7 8 9 10   REL   13 12 11

# Table of Contents

## Personal Finance Activity 1
# Balancing Your Checkbook

**ACTIVITY GOAL**

This Personal Finance Activity will teach you to balance a checking account. It will demonstrate the use of a check register and banking statement. You will learn that some withdrawals from your account are immediate while others take time to process.

**DIRECTIONS:** *Recording transactions in your check register completely and immediately will help you better track your money. To make sure that you and your bank have not made any mistakes, it is important to balance your account each month. Your bank will probably send you a monthly statement with a worksheet to help you balance your account. Many banks also provide statements online as well. Look at the partial check register below. Then review the bank summary on the next page. Use the following steps and the worksheet on page four to balance this checking account.*

| Check Register | | | | | | |
|---|---|---|---|---|---|---|
| CHECK NUMBER | DATE | TRANSACTION DESCRIPTION | PAYMENT AMOUNT | √ | DEPOSIT AMOUNT | BALANCE |
| | 9-1 | Balance brought forward | | √ | | $2,058.62 |
| 1271 | 9-10 | Mayfield Bank (auto pmt.) | 124.66 | | | 1,933.96 |
| | 9-15 | Deposit (paycheck) | | | 342.77 | 2,276.73 |
| | 9-22 | ATM withdrawal – Locust St. | 20.00 | | | 2,256.73 |
| 1272 | 9-25 | Bally's Music Store | 28.72 | | | 2,228.01 |
| 1273 | 9-29 | Quest Wireless Co | 34.99 | | | 2,193.02 |
| | 9-30 | Debit card – J.B. Grocer | 15.18 | | | 2,177.84 |
| | 10-1 | Deposit (paycheck) | | | 342.77 | 2,520.61 |
| | 10-5 | Deposit (gift from Aunt Eva) | | | 50.00 | 2,570.61 |
| | 10-5 | Withdrawal - transfer to savings | 100.00 | | | 2,470.61 |
| 1274 | 10-6 | Adam's Bike Shop | 22.38 | | | 2,448.23 |

## Personal Finance Activity 1 *(continued)*

**Checking Account Summary from 9/1 to 9/30**
**Account #123-456789**

| 9/1 | **Beginning Balance** | **$2,058.62** |
|---|---|---|
| 2 | Checks | $(153.38) |
| 2 | Withdrawals/Debits | $(35.18) |
| 1 | Deposits/Credits | $342.77 |
| **9/30** | **Ending Balance** | **$2,212.83** |

**CHECKS**

| Check # | Date Paid | Amount |
|---|---|---|
| 1271 | 9/13 | 124.66 |
| 1272 | 9/27 | 28.72 |

**WITHDRAWALS/DEBITS**

| Date | Amount | Description |
|---|---|---|
| 9/22 | 20.00 | ATM at 1582 Locust St. |
| 9/30 | 15.18 | Debit Card purchase at J.B. Grocer |

**DEPOSITS**

| Date | Amount | Description |
|---|---|---|
| 9/15 | 342.77 | Direct Payroll Deposit, Acct. 0023*****723 |

**Step 1:** Compare the check register to the bank checking account summary. Look in the Checks section of the account summary. Note that checks 1271 and 1272 are listed in this section. Place a checkmark in the appropriate column of the check register for each of these checks. The checkmarks in your register will remind you that these checks have been received by the bank and the amounts have been taken out of your account.

**Step 2:** Look at the Withdrawals/Debit section of the summary. Find these transactions in the check register and put checkmarks next to them.

**Step 3:** Look at the Deposits section of the summary. Find the deposit in the check register and put a checkmark next to it.

## Personal Finance Activity 1 (continued)

**Step 4:** Note the transactions in your check register that do not have checkmarks next to them. Although the bank statement covers dates from 9-1 to 9-30, the check written on 9-29 is not shown on the statement. Explain why you think it is not shown.

_____

_____

_____

_____

**Step 5:** Look at the Worksheet to Balance a Checking Account on the next page. The first line asks for the ending balance from your statement or summary. Find that balance on the bank summary and write it on line 1 of the worksheet.

**Step 6:** Find the deposits in the check register that do not have checkmarks next to them. Enter the date and the amount of each of these deposits in the second section of the worksheet. Write the total of these deposits on line 2.

**Step 7:** Add line 1 to line 2. Place the total on line 3 of the worksheet.

**Step 8:** In the check register, find the checks, debit card transactions, and other withdrawals that do not have checkmarks next to them. Enter the information for each in the fourth section of the worksheet. Write the total of these transactions on line 4.

**Step 9:** Subtract line 4 from line 3. Does this amount equal the balance shown on the last row of the check register? If so, you have successfully balanced this account.

**Step 10:** Sometimes accounts do not balance on the first try. What things can you recheck if your account does not balance?

_____

_____

_____

_____

## Personal Finance Activity 1 (continued)

### Worksheet to Balance a Checking Account

1.  Enter the ending balance from your statement _____ (1) $_____

2.  List deposits and credits made after statement date.

| Date | Amount | Date | Amount |
|------|--------|------|--------|
|      |        |      |        |
|      |        |      |        |
|      |        |      |        |

Enter the total of above deposits and credits.                  (2) $_____

3.  Subtotal line (1) + line (2)                                 (3) $_____

4.  List checks, debit card transactions, and other withdrawals
    not shown on the statement.

| Check #/Date | Amount | Check #/Date | Amount |
|--------------|--------|--------------|--------|
|              |        |              |        |
|              |        |              |        |
|              |        |              |        |
|              |        |              |        |

Enter total of all checks, debits, and withdrawals above.       (4) $_____

5.  Subtract line (4) from line (3)
    This should be your present account balance.                 (5) $_____

## Personal Finance Activity 2
# Tracking Your Spending

$

### ACTIVITY GOAL

This Personal Finance Activity will help you consider your own spending habits. It will also give you a chance to look at another person's habits. Helping someone improve their budgeting may help you look at your own spending habits more objectively.

**DIRECTIONS:** *A budget allows you to look at your spending versus income. If the amount of spending is more than you earn, changes need to be made. In this activity, you will evaluate a student's budget and make suggestions to improve his spending and saving habits. The student tracked all of his purchases for one month the following chart. He works 12 hours per week, earning a net pay of $7 per hour. His parents also give him $15 each week for school lunches. Using this information, answer the questions below.*

| Week No. | Items Purchased | Cost |
|---|---|---|
| Week 1 | Lunches—$2.50 × 5 lunches | $ 12.50 |
| | Vending machine (pop and snacks)—$1 × 5 days | 5.00 |
| | Movie and snacks at theater | 12.00 |
| | 2 books | 24.00 |
| | Shoes | 38.00 |
| | Paid Mom and Dad for gasoline used in their car | 8.00 |
| Week 2 | Lunches—$2.50 × 5 lunches | 12.50 |
| | Vending machine (pop and snacks)—$1 × 5 days | 5.00 |
| | Dinner at restaurant | 7.00 |
| | Video game | 35.00 |
| | Paid Mom and Dad for gasoline used in their car | 12.00 |
| Week 3 | Lunches—$2.50 × 5 lunches | 12.50 |
| | Vending machine (pop and snacks)—$1 × 5 days | 5.00 |
| | 2 music CDs | 28.00 |
| | Sweater ($46) and jeans ($62) | 108.00 |
| | Paid Mom and Dad for gasoline used in their car | 10.00 |
| Week 4 | Lunches—$2.50 × 5 lunches | 12.50 |
| | Vending machine (pop and snacks)—$1 × 5 days | 5.00 |
| | Paid cell phone bill ($34 for monthly bill + $15 for using extra minutes) | 49.00 |
| | Dinner at restaurant | 8.50 |
| | Movie and snacks at theater | 11.00 |
| | Music CD | 15.00 |
| | Paid Mom and Dad for gasoline used in their car | 8.00 |

## Personal Finance Activity 2 *(continued)*

1.  How much did the student spend this month? What is his total income for the month?

    _____

2.  Are the student's income sources or expenses higher? Is this student doing a good job budgeting his money? Explain your answer.

    _____

    _____

3.  Are there any items that the student might have paid too much for because of advertising? Explain your answer.

    _____

    _____

4.  Are there any items that could be considered impulse purchases? Explain your answer.

    _____

    _____

    _____

5.  If this student were to ask you for advice related to his budget, what would you tell him?

    _____

    _____

    _____

6.  Can you think of a way for this student to better track his spending, savings, and income?

    _____

    _____

    _____

**Personal Finance Activities** 6

Name _____ Date _____ Class _____

## Personal Finance Activity 3
# Risk and Return

**ACTIVITY GOAL**

This Personal Finance Activity will help you compare and contrast many types of investments. You will explain the advantages and disadvantages of some investments and calculate the earnings of a savings account and a stock.

**DIRECTIONS:** *Whether your investments are big or small, you should choose the investment that best suits you. Consider the risks involved, the earnings potential, and whether you can withdraw your money without a penalty. In this activity, you will take a look at a stock and compare its earnings to those you might get from a savings account.*

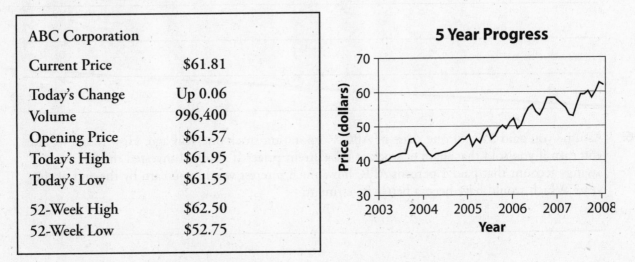

| ABC Corporation | |
|---|---|
| Current Price | $61.81 |
| Today's Change | Up 0.06 |
| Volume | 996,400 |
| Opening Price | $61.57 |
| Today's High | $61.95 |
| Today's Low | $61.55 |
| 52-Week High | $62.50 |
| 52-Week Low | $52.75 |

**5 Year Progress**

1. What is the current price of one share of stock for ABC Corporation?

_____

2. What was the highest price in the last year? What was the lowest price in the last year?

_____

_____

3. How does the current price compare to the highest and lowest prices of the last year?

_____

_____

## Personal Finance Activity 3 *(continued)*

**4.** Use the line chart to determine the approximate price of the stock at the beginning of 2003. How much money would you have earned if you bought one share of stock at the beginning of 2003 and sold it at today's current price?

_____

_____

**5.** Assume the chart showing the growth of this stock over five years is typical for most stocks. What does it tell you about investing in stock for a short time period versus a longer time?

_____

_____

_____

**6.** Assume you paid $57 for one share of ABC Corporation stock one year ago. How much would you earn if you sold that share of stock at the current price? If you had invested the $57 in a savings account that paid 1 percent APR, how much interest would you earn by the end of the year? Which would have been a better investment?

_____

_____

_____

**7.** Compare investing in stocks to depositing your money in a savings account. Discuss the risk and return associated with each.

_____

_____

_____

Name _____ Date _____ Class _____

## Personal Finance Activity 4
# Comparing Credit Card Offers

**ACTIVITY GOAL**

This Personal Finance Activity will help you compare different credit card offers. Understanding the details of each credit card plan will help you make intelligent decisions about what type of card to use and how best to manage your financial debts.

**DIRECTIONS:** *To properly compare the advantages and disadvantages of each credit card offer, you need to make a careful comparison of the features each card offers. Use the chart below to find the information that answers the following series of questions about each card. When you are done with each step, you will have the information needed to make an informed decision about which credit card is right for your needs and financial situation.*

| Comparing Two Credit Card Offers | |
|---|---|
| Credit Card A | Credit Card B |
| 3.99% APR for the life of transferred balances; 13.25 % APR for all other purchases | 0.00% APR for 6 months; 19.8% APR for remaining lifetime of card |
| $50 annual fee; $25 fee for late payments | No annual fee; $25 fee for late payments |
| Minimum monthly payment of $15 or 10% of balance | Monthly balance must be paid in full each month |
| Set your own payment date | Must pay card by the 15th day of the month |
| Rewards program: $10 shopping card with each $1,000 in spending | Rewards program: Earn 1% cash back on all purchases |

**Step 1:** What is the Annual Percentage Rate (APR) of credit card A and credit card B?

_____

_____

_____

## Personal Finance Activity 4 *(continued)*

**Step 2:** a) What are other fees associated with each credit card?
b) How do these fees impact your total monthly bill?

_____

_____

_____

**Step 3:** What are the requirements for paying your credit card each month?

_____

_____

_____

**Step 4:** What would the minimum monthly payment be for each credit card for balances of $15, $130, $180, and $300?

_____

_____

**Step 5:** a) What benefits or rewards does each card offer to make it more attractive for the consumer?
b) How do these characteristics affect your evaluation of each card?

_____

_____

**Step 6:** If you have a fixed amount of income each month and your expenses are very close in dollar amount to your income, which of these two credit card offers would be a safer choice? Explain your answer.

_____

_____

_____

Name_____ Date_____ Class _____

**ACTIVITY GOAL**

This Personal Finance Activity will help you evaluate what type of college best fits your needs. You will be asked to consider the field you'd like to enter, to think about the cost, size, and location of a school, and to consider the financial aid that is available.

**DIRECTIONS:** *Choosing a college takes a lot of research and thought. Many factors must be considered since your college education will likely play a major role in your future. The chart below compares some of the factors for four schools. Use the information to answer the following questions.*

| | School A | School B | School C | School D |
|---|---|---|---|---|
| **Field of Study** | Offers a four-year degree in your field of study; school's program for your field has an excellent reputation | Offers a four-year degree in your field of study | Offers a four-year degree in your field of study | Offers a four-year degree in your field of study; school's program for your field has an excellent reputation |
| **No. of Students** | 16,000 | 37,000 | 6,300 | 6,700 |
| **Public or Private** | Public | Public | Private | Private |
| **Annual Tuition In-State Out-of-State** | $11,863 $22,988 | $8,667 $20,562 | $23,140 $23,140 | $22,635 $22,635 |
| **Room & Board** | $8,140 | $7,236 | $6,600 | $7,060 |
| **Location** | Out of State: Five-hour drive from your home | In-State: Two-hour drive from your home | Out-of-State: Eight-hour drive from your home | In-State: 30-minute drive from your home |
| **Financial Aid Available** | $3,000 grant $8,000 scholarship $10,000 loan work study available | $3,000 grant $4,000 scholarship $8,000 loan work study available | $1,700 grant $12,000 scholarship $10,000 loan | $500 grant $10,000 scholarship $13,000 loan |

1. What are the total costs for tuition and room and board of each school? Be sure to factor in the location of each school.

_____

_____

_____

_____

## Personal Finance Activity 5 *(continued)*                                    (\$)

2.  When you subtract the financial aid from the costs above, how much additional money will you need to cover the expenses for the first year at each school?

    _____

    _____

    _____

3.  Describe the differences between the public schools and the private schools listed. Consider the size of the school, tuition costs, and financial aid offers.

    _____

    _____

    _____

    _____

4.  Since School D is only a 30-minute drive from home, a student could live at home and drive or take public transportation to school. List some of the advantages and disadvantages of commuting.

    _____

    _____

    _____

5.  Overall, which school is most appealing to you? Explain your answer in detail.

    _____

    _____

    _____

    _____

## Personal Finance Activity 6
# Preparing for an Interview

**ACTIVITY GOAL**

This Personal Finance Activity will help you prepare for an interview. Preparing for questions that an interviewer might ask and questions that you would like to ask means a lot to most employers. It might just give you an advantage over your competition

**DIRECTIONS:** *As you begin working, you will probably find that enjoying your job is just as important as the money you earn. Finding a job that interests you is the first step. The next step is landing the job. How you act in an interview will have a big impact on whether you are awarded the job. Before getting started, think of a job that interests you. If you cannot think of one on your own, pick one from the list below. The questions that follow are ones that might be asked during the interview process. Write your answers to the questions to help you prepare for your interviews.*

❖ Working as a salesperson at a clothing, electronics, music, or other retail store
❖ Delivering meals to shut-ins
❖ Working at a home for the elderly
❖ Reading to children at a library
❖ Becoming a camp counselor or helper at an after-school daycare
❖ Delivering newspapers
❖ Working at a restaurant as a hostess, waiter or waitress, or cook
❖ Becoming a lifeguard
❖ Operating rides at an amusement park
❖ Doing yard work for a landscaping company
❖ Conducting customer surveys at a local mall
❖ Assisting an office manager by answering telephones and typing correspondences

1. What can you tell me about yourself?

_____

_____

_____

2. Why do you want this job?

_____

_____

_____

## Personal Finance Activity 6 (continued)

**3.** What are your greatest strengths? What are your greatest weaknesses?

_____

_____

_____

**4.** What skills, characteristics, or experience do you possess that will help you in this job?

_____

_____

_____

**5.** Describe a time when you worked with a difficult person. How did you handle it? Do you think you should have done anything differently?

_____

_____

_____

_____

**6.** Where do you see yourself in five years? In ten years?

_____

_____

_____

**7.** List some questions you might ask your potential employer during an interview.

_____

_____

_____

_____

## Personal Finance Activity 7
# Understanding Your Paycheck

### ACTIVITY GOAL

This Personal Finance Activity will help you better understand how taxes and other deductions affect your earnings. After completing the activity, you will be able to calculate earnings and understand items shown on a paycheck stub.

**DIRECTIONS:** *The difference between the gross pay and net pay an employee earns can be substantial. You have learned that taxes and other deductions are taken out of an employee's gross pay, changing the amount that the employee actually receives. In this activity, you will analyze the earnings and some typical deductions found on a paycheck stub.*

| Earnings | Rate($/hr) | Hours | Current Period | Year to Date |
|---|---|---|---|---|
| Regular | 10.00 | 32 | 320.00 | 15,645.00 |
| Overtime | 15.00 | 0 | 0.00 | 97.50 |
| **GROSS PAY** | | | **$320.00** | **$15,742.50** |
| **Deductions** | | | | |
| Federal Income Tax | | | 16.00 | 787.13 |
| Social Security Tax | | | 19.84 | 976.04 |
| State Income Tax | | | 11.20 | 550.99 |
| City Income Tax | | | 4.80 | 236.14 |
| 401(K) | | | 12.80 | 629.70 |
| Life Insurance | | | 4.84 | 238.11 |
| Medical Insurance | | | 13.29 | 653.80 |
| **NET PAY** | | | **$237.23** | **$11,670.59** |

1. Explain what the terms "Current Period" and "Year to Date" mean on this pay stub.

_____

_____

_____

2. What amount of net pay has been earned this period? What amount has been earned since January 1?

_____

_____

**Personal Finance Activity 7** *(continued)*

3. What amount of gross pay has been earned this period? What amount has been earned since January 1?

   _____

   _____

4. What is the difference (in dollors) between the gross pay and net pay for this pay period?

   _____

5. What percentage of the gross pay will this employee take home? How did you calculate your answer?

   _____

   _____

6. Which of the deductions listed are required by law? Which are usually optional to the employee?

   _____

   _____

   _____

7. Which deductions do you think change depending upon the amount of gross pay? Which remain the same each pay period regardless of the amount of pay? Explain your answer.

   _____

   _____

   _____

   _____

8. Assuming the overtime rate has not changed, how many hours of overtime has this employee worked so far this year? How did you calculate your answer?

   _____

   _____

   _____

**Personal Finance Activities** 16

## Personal Finance Activity 8
# Finding Your First Apartment

**ACTIVITY GOAL**

This Personal Finance Activity will help you compare different features of apartments for rent. Since you'll be required to sign a lease when renting an apartment, you'll need to make a decision that you will be happy with for many months to come.

**DIRECTIONS:** *Assume that you are starting a new year at college and would like to rent a nearby apartment. You find the ads below in a local newspaper. Analyze each advertisement and then complete the following steps to determine which apartment would be the most affordable one to rent.*

| | | |
|---|---|---|
| **Maplewood** - clean 1BR/ 1BA. Full kitchen. Wash/ dry in unit. Short walk to campus. Pets under 25 lbs okay. $425/mo, utilities included. 1 mo security deposit required. 9 mo lease. | **Maplewood** - 2 BR/1.5 BA. $600 rent, utils pd. Walk to campus. Coin lndry on site. No pets. 1 year lease. 1 mo deposit. | **West Maplewood** - Lg 2BR/2BA. On busline. 4 mi to campus. Balcony. Pool. Pets okay. $400 rent + 2 mo deposit. $150 utilities/mo. 9 mo lease. No laundry. |

**STEP 1:** Identify all of the abbreviations used in the ads. What do they mean?

_____

**STEP 2:** Identify which apartment seems to be the most affordable.

_____

| | Expense | Apartment 1 | Apartment 2 | Apartment 3 |
|---|---|---|---|---|
| A | Rent | | | |
| B | Utilities | | | |
| C | Total Cost per Month | | | |
| D | Total Cost per Person per Month | | | |
| | | | | |
| E | Total Security Deposit | | | |
| F | Security Deposit per Person | | | |
| G | Cost per Person for First Month Only | | | |
| H | Cost per Person for Eight Months | | | |
| I | Total Cost per Person for School Year (nine months) | | | |

## Personal Finance Activity 8 *(continued)* $\$$

**Step 3:** On Line A and Line B of the chart on the previous page, write the cost of the rent and utilities for each apartment.

**Step 4:** Add the rent and utilities together and write the totals on Line C of the chart.

**Step 5:** Assume that you would live alone in a one-bedroom apartment and you would have a roommate if you rented a two-bedroom apartment. Figure out what the total rent and utilities would be per person. Write the amounts on Line D.

**Step 6:** What is the total security deposit for each apartment? Write the amounts on Line E of the chart.

**Step 7:** Figure out how much the security deposit would be for each person and write the amounts on Line F.

**Step 8:** Add the security deposit per person to the total cost per person per month. Write the amounts on Line G to show how much money you would need to pay the first month of your rental.

**Step 9:** Calculate how much each person would have to pay over the next eight months to rent each apartment. Write the amounts on Line H. Remember that the security deposit is only paid during the first month.

**Step 10:** Add the totals for the first month to the totals for the remaining eight months. Write the sum on Line I to show what your total cost would be to live in each apartment during a nine-month school term.

**Step 11:** Look at your answer for Step 2. Is the most affordable apartment the same as what you answered in that step?

_____

_____

**Step 12:** Aside from the costs calculated above, list other factors that would make you choose one of these apartments over the other two.

_____

_____

_____

Name_____ Date_____ Class_____

# Financing a Car

**ACTIVITY GOAL**

This Personal Finance Activity will help you analyze several different factors that affect what you pay when you finance a vehicle. You will learn more about interest rates and other terms of automobile loans.

**DIRECTIONS:** *Many factors affect the amount that you will pay when purchasing a car. Assume that you are financing a new car and three different financial institutions have given you the financing options in the chart below. Answer the questions below to determine the advantages and disadvantages of financing with each institution.*

|  | Financing Option 1 | Financing Option 2 | Financing Option 3 |
|---|---|---|---|
| **Price of Vehicle (including tax, title, registration, and fees)** | $18,445 | $18,445 | $18,445 |
| **Down Payment** | $1,000 | $1,000 | $1,000 |
| **Amount to be Financed** | $17,445 | $17,445 | $17,445 |
| **Annual Percentage Rate (APR)** | 4.9% | 0% | 2.9% |
| **Life of Loan** | 60 months | 36 months | 48 months |
| **Monthly Payment** | $328.41 | $484.58 | $385.36 |

1. What is the Annual Percentage Rate (APR) offered for each financing option?

   _____

   _____

   _____

2. Is there any correlation between the APR and the life of the loan?

   _____

   _____

3. Which financing option offers the lowest monthly payment?

   _____

## Personal Finance Activity 9 (continued)

**4.** What is the total price you will pay using each option? (Hint: Multiply the monthly payment by the total number of months you will pay.)

_____

**5.** Which option offers the lowest total price? Is this option the same as the option with the lowest monthly payment? Explain why this is the case.

_____

_____

_____

**6.** Discuss the advantages and disadvantages of each option. Be sure to include information about each APR, life of the loan, monthly payment, and total price you will pay over the life of the loan.

_____

_____

_____

_____

**7.** When you lease a car, you finance the use of the car for a specific amount of time. When that time period ends, you return the car to the dealer. Assume you can lease the same car in the above example for $225.00 per month for 48 months. How much would you pay over the four years? How does this total cost compare with the least expensive purchase option?

_____

_____

**8.** What advantages and disadvantages do you see to leasing a car?

_____

_____

_____

_____

Name_____ Date_____ Class_____

**ACTIVITY GOAL**

This Personal Finance Activity will allow you to take a more detailed look at medical, car, property, and life insurance. Learning more about insurance will allow you to make better informed decisions about your personal needs.

**DIRECTIONS:** *Assume that your employer offers two medical insurance plans to full-time employees. Both plans provide excellent coverage. The details of each plan are outlined in the table below. Use this information to answer the questions that follow.*

|  | Health Care Plan A | Health Care Plan B |
|---|---|---|
| **CO-PAYS AND DEDUCTIBLES** | | |
| **Co-pay for office visit with primary care physician** | $10 | $25 |
| **Co-pay for office visit with specialist** | $25 | $35 |
| **Co-pay for emergency room visit** | $40 (refunded if admitted to hospital) | $50 (refunded if admitted to hospital) |
| **Co-pay for hospital visit** | $75 | $100 |
| **Annual deductible** | none | 20% deductible for surgery only; maximum annual deductible, $400 |
| **Co-pay for level 1 prescriptions** | $10 | $25 |
| **Co-pay for level 2 prescriptions** | $25 | $40 |
| **Co-pay for level 3 prescriptions** | $40 | $50 |
| **Vision plan co-pays** | $20 co-pay for exams; you pay 80% of cost of supplies | no vision plan available |
| **MONTHLY COSTS PAID BY EMPLOYEE** | | |
| **Single coverage** | $50 | $35 |
| **Employee + spouse** | $110 | $75 |
| **Family** | $160 | $105 |
| **MONTHLY COSTS PAID BY EMPLOYER** | | |
| **Single coverage** | $200 | $200 |
| **Employee + spouse** | $350 | $350 |
| **Family** | $500 | $500 |

**Personal Finance Activity 10** *(continued)*                                   $

1. What is the difference between a deductible and a co-pay?

_____

_____

_____

2. What amounts would an employee have to pay for each of the following services? Write the amounts in the following table.

| Service | Cost Before Insurance | Cost Using Plan A | Cost Using Plan B |
|---|---|---|---|
| Appointment with primary doctor to treat a sore throat | $85 | | |
| Purchasing a prescription for an antibiotic (level 1 prescription) | $120 | | |
| Annual eye exam | $65 | | |
| Purchase of eyeglasses | $230 | | |
| Visit to a dermatologist (specialist) | $115 | | |
| Annual total for allergy medicine (12 prescriptions, each level 2) | $900 | | |
| Visit to the ER; immediately admitted to the hospital for one night | $1,200 | | |
| Out-patient knee surgery | $4,700 | | |
| **Total Costs** | | | |

3. Calculate the total cost for each column of the above table. Write the totals in the last row.

4. How much does the employee save using Plan A? Using Plan B?

_____

_____

5. Most employees pay for a portion of their health insurance by having the cost deducted from each paycheck. Most employers pay for a portion of the cost as well. If an employee chooses the Employee + Spouse option (see table on page 21), how much does this employer pay over the course of a year? How did you calculate your answer?

_____

_____

**Personal Finance Activity 10** *(continued)*

6. If an employee uses the Employee + Spouse option for Plan A, how much would be deducted from his paycheck in one year? How much would be deducted for Plan B?

_____

_____

7. If this same employee incurred the medical costs listed on the previous page over one year, which health care plan would provide greater benefit to him? Be sure to consider the cost of the insurance and the total co-pays, deductibles, and other medical expenses paid using each plan. Explain your answer.

_____

_____

_____

_____

_____

8. If an employee seldom incurs medical costs, would they benefit most from Plan A or from Plan B? Explain your answer.

_____

_____

_____

_____

9. Considering the costs that you have calculated while answering these questions, explain how you feel about health insurance. Is it necessary? Is it worth the up-front costs?

_____

_____

_____

_____

# Answer Key

## Activity 1: Balancing Your Checkbook

**4.** The check written on 9-29 does not appear on the bank statement because the bank did not receive and clear the check by 9-30. Processing of the check may take a few days.

**9.** Final worksheet should include these figures:

**Worksheet to Balance a Checking Account**

1. Enter the ending balance from your statement — (1) $ 2,212.83

2. List deposits and credits made after statement date.

| Date | Amount | Date | Amount |
|------|--------|------|--------|
| 10-1 | 342.77 | | |
| 10-5 | 50.00 | | |
| | | | |

Enter the total of above deposits and credits. — (2) $ 392.77

3. Subtotal line (1) + line (2) — (3) $ 2,605.60

4. List checks, debit card transactions, and other withdrawals not shown on the statement.

| Check #/Date | Amount | Check #/Date | Amount |
|--------------|--------|--------------|--------|
| 1273/9-29 | 34.99 | | |
| 10-5 | 100.00 | | |
| 1274/10-6 | 22.38 | | |
| | | | |

Enter total of all checks, debits, and withdrawals above. — (4) $ 157.37

5. Subtract line (4) from line (3)
This should be your present account balance. — (5) $ 2,448.23

**10.** Students' answers may include one or more of the following ideas: check the accuracy of the math you used to calculate the balance after each transaction; make sure that deposits are added to the balance and withdrawals are subtracted; make sure all outstanding checks, withdrawals, debits, and deposits are listed; check for missing preauthorized/automatic deductions or deposits; check for missing ATM and debit card transactions; make sure all bank charges are entered into the register; if the account earns interest, make sure it was added to the register.

## Activity 2: Practicing the Skill

**1.** The student spent $443.50. His income was $396.00 ($7 per hour × 48 hours per month = $336.00; $15 allowance × 4 = $60.00; $336.00 + $60.00 = $396.00).

**2.** The student's expenses are higher than his income. Answers should state that this student is not doing a good job of budgeting; not only will he run out of money each month, but he is not saving any money and is probably making some unnecessary purchases.

**3.** Answers will vary. The student may have overspent on clothing due to advertising of brand names.

**4.** Vending machine snacks, snacks at the theater, video games, music CDs, and even clothing may have been impulse purchases. These are items the student may not have really needed.

**5.** Students' answers will vary but may include that money could be saved by avoiding unnecessary purchases and overpriced items. The student could also cut down on snacks or bring snacks from home. The student should also consider tracking the minutes he uses on his cell phone; extra minutes beyond what his plan covers are expensive. This student should also be saving part of his income

**6.** Students might suggest a budget sheet similar to the one in the Personal Finance Handbook that categorizes types of spending and lists income and savings. Other students may suggest their own method of tracking money, such as using envelopes to hold money budgeted for various items.

## Activity 3: Risk and Return

**1.** $61.81
**2.** $62.50; $52.75
**3.** The current price is $.69 lower than the highest price of the year and $9.06 higher than the lowest price of the year.
**4.** The approximate price of the stock at the beginning of 2003 was $39. One would earn $22.81 if the stock was sold at the current price.
**5.** The chart demonstrates that if a stock is held for a long period of time, gains are often steady and sometimes substantial. For any short period of time, ups and downs are common and will result in inconsistent earnings.

6. Stock earnings on the ABC Corporation stock would be $4.81. Savings account earnings would be $.57. The stock would have been the better investment.

7. As shown in the previous example, stocks often offer a higher return on your investment, but they are much riskier; the return is not guaranteed. A savings account is much safer but returns can be significantly lower.

## Activity 4: Comparing Credit Card Offers

1. The APR for Credit Card A is 3.99% for all transferred balances and 13.25% for all other purchases. The APR for Credit Card B is 0% for the first six months and 19.8% for purchases after that time.

2. a) Fees associated with Card A include an annual fee of $50 and a $25 fee each for late payment. Fees associated with Card B include only a $25 fee for each late payment. b) Most annual fees are paid in a lump sum on your first statement; the next annual fee will not be charged for another year. Late fees are only charged if your payment is late (or beyond the grace period). Some students may note that although Card A has a higher annual fee, the APR is lower. Since both of these factors affect the total monthly bill, some who carry a high balance each month might benefit from the features of Card A.

3. Card A requires the owner to pay at least $15 or 10% of the balance, whichever is higher. Card B requires the entire balance to be paid each month.

4. The minimum payments for the cards would be as follows:

| Balance | Card A Minimum Payment | Card B Minimum Payment |
|---|---|---|
| $15 | $15 | $15 |
| $130 | $15 | $130 |
| $180 | $18 | $180 |
| $300 | $30 | $300 |

5. a) Each card essentially offers a 1% reward on all purchases. b) The difference lies in how that 1% is paid. Card A pays a $10 shopping card for each $1,000 in spending (1% of $1,000 = $10). Card B pays cash back. Many consumers would prefer Card B for two reasons. First, most prefer cash over a shopping card that you might be able to use only with specific merchants. Second, Card B gives 1% back on every purchase; Card A would require you to reach a $1,000 increment in spending before issuing a shopping card.

6. Answers will vary. Credit Card B is the safer of the two cards. Although it has a higher APR, students should realize that if their income and expenses are nearly equal, they should pay off the balance every month anyway. Card B requires you to pay the entire balance, thus avoiding the temptation of the credit card trap.

## Activity 5: Choosing the Right School for You

1. A: $31,128; B: $15,903; C: $29,740; D: $29,695.

2. A: $10,128; B: $903; C: $6,040; D: $6,195

3. The private schools have fewer students. Although the in-state tuition for the public schools is significantly lower than that for the private schools, the out-of-state tuition for all four schools is close in price. The tuition of the private schools does not change if a student lives out of the state. Both private schools offer more financial aid (especially in scholarships, which are not repaid); however, School A offers only a few thousand less.

4. Advantages: Students could live with their parents and save room and board costs. Students may remain in a familiar environment. Disadvantages: Reliable transportation, weather, and traffic could affect the commute. Transportation can be costly. Students miss the college experience of living away from parents.

5. Students' answers will vary greatly depending on what they are looking for in a college. The size of the school, preference of private vs. public, opinion on going to a school that specializes in their field, distance from home,

financial considerations, and other factors will influence their decisions.

## Activity 6: Preparing for an Interview

1. Students' answers will vary greatly. They may choose to discuss previous work experience, personal characteristics, participation in clubs or sports, school subjects in which they are interested, or personal interests and hobbies. Students may mention personal interests but should focus on information that relates to their qualifications for employment.

2. Students' answers will vary. They may include that they would enjoy the nature of the job; their skills, experience, or characteristics will help them succeed in the job; or they would be a positive contribution to the company.

3. Students' answers will vary. Possible strengths include dependability, work ethic, ability to get along with others, leadership qualities, problem-solving abilities, positive attitude, ability to work under pressure or to focus, and professional expertise. Students should use common sense when identifying weaknesses. The weakness should be minor and students should identify how they are working to overcome the weaknesses. Another appropriate response could be "overdoing" what is usually viewed as a positive characteristic. For instance, a student could answer that they are a bit of a perfectionist.

4. Students' answers will vary depending on their skills, characteristics, experience, and how they relate to the job they have chosen.

5. Students' answers will vary depending on their experiences, but they may cite an example in a previous job or a classroom setting.

6. Some students will state that they will be in college five years from now. They should give a more descriptive answer, including what they plan to study and how they hope to accomplish personal goals. In 10 years, most should answer according to a career goal that they have in mind.

7. Students should realize the importance of asking questions during an interview and list several questions. They could include: Could you provide more detail on the daily activities of this position? What are the typical working hours for this position? Could you describe a typical day for this position? What advancement opportunities are available? How will my performance be evaluated and by whom? Is on-the-job training available? What are the organization's strengths and weaknesses compared to the competition?

## Activity 7: Understanding Your Paycheck

1. Current Period refers to the most recent pay period. Year to Date refers to the amount of pay or deductions made from January 1 of the current year until now.

2. Current net pay is $237.23. Since January 1, $11,670.59 has been earned.

3. Current gross pay is $320.00. Since January 1, $15,742.50 has been earned.

4. $82.77

5. The employee will take home 74.13 percent of his gross pay. The answer is calculated by using the formula: 237.23 (net pay) ÷ 320 (gross pay).

6. The federal income tax, social security tax, state income tax, and city income tax (depending on city) are required to be paid by law. Participation in (thus deductions for) 401K plans and life and medical insurance are usually optional.

7. The deductions for federal income tax, social security tax, state income tax, city income tax, and 401K vary depending on the gross pay because they are calculated as a percentage of the gross pay. Life and medical insurance payments usually remain consistent regardless of pay.

8. The employee has worked 6.5 hours of overtime. This result is calculated by using the formula: 97.50 (year-to-date pay) ÷ 15 (rate of overtime pay).

## Activity 8: Finding Your First Apartment

1. BR/BA—bedroom/bathroom; wash/dry—washer & dryer; lbs—pounds; mo—month; utils—utilities; lndry—laundry; lg—large; mi—miles.

**2.** If students factor in that they could share a two-bedroom apartment with a roommate, they may pick the third apartment. If they do not factor in a roommate, they may pick the first apartment.

| | Expense | Apartment 1 | Apartment 2 | Apartment 3 |
|---|---|---|---|---|
| A | Rent | $425 | $600 | $400 |
| B | Utilities | 0 | 0 | 150 |
| C | Total Cost per Month | 425 | 600 | 550 |
| D | Total Cost per Person per Month | 425 | 300 | 275 |
| E | Total Security Deposit | 425 | 600 | 800 |
| F | Security Deposit per Person | 425 | 300 | 400 |
| G | Cost per Person for First Month Only | 850 | 600 | 675 |
| H | Cost per Person for Eight Months | 3,400 | 2,400 | 2,200 |
| I | Total Cost per Person for School Year (9 months) | 4,250 | 3,000 | 2,875 |

**11.** Answers will vary depending on students' answers to Step 2.

**12.** Other factors to consider include desire to have a roommate, amenities (such as laundry facilities and cost, pool, and balcony), proximity to campus, and length of lease (a one-year lease will run past the school year).

## Activity 9: Financing a Car

**1.** Option 1: 4.9 percent; Option 2: 0 percent; Option 3: 2.9 percent

**2.** In these examples, the APR is lower for shorter-term loans and is higher for longer-term loans.

**3.** Option 1 offers the lowest monthly payment.

**4.** Option 1: $19,704.60; Option 2: $17,444.88; Option 3: $18,497.28

**5.** Option 2 offers the lowest total price. It is not the same as the option with the lowest monthly payment. The difference results from a lower interest rate and fewer payments.

**6.** Option 1 offers the lowest monthly payments so it might be most affordable on a short-term basis. However, since it has a higher interest rate and more payments, it is the most expensive option in the long run. Option 2 has the highest monthly payment, so it might be too expensive for some. Because of the 0 percent interest rate and lower number of payments, it is the least expensive in the long run. Option 3 falls in the middle; all factors fall between the other two options.

**7.** $10,800. This is $6,644.88 cheaper than Option 2.

**8.** There are many pros and cons to leasing a car. Given the information provided, students should at least realize that lease payments are much lower, but they do not get to keep the car once the lease is over. If they continue to lease cars, they will always have a monthly payment. However, if they purchase a car, they can own it long after they quit making payments.

## Activity 10: The Need for Insurance

**1.** A deductible is the amount that you must pay in full before insurance pays anything. Many deductibles are stated in annual terms; once you reach the deductible amount for the year, insurance pays the rest. A new deductible applies to the next year. A co-pay is a payment you must make each time an event occurs, such as visiting a doctor or filling a prescription.

**2.**

| Service | Cost Before Insurance | Cost Using Plan A | Cost Using Plan B |
|---|---|---|---|
| Appointment with primary doctor to treat a sore throat | $85 | $10 | $25 |
| Purchasing a pre-scription for an antibiotic (level 1 prescription) | $120 | $10 | $25 |
| Annual eye exam | $65 | $20 | $65 |
| Purchase of eyeglasses | $230 | $184 | $230 |
| Visit to a dermatolo-gist (specialist) | $115 | $25 | $35 |
| Annual total for allergy medicine (12 prescriptions, each level 2) | $900 | $300 | $480 |
| Visit to the ER; immediately admit-ted to the hospital for one night | $1,200 | $75 | $100 |
| Out-patient knee surgery | $4,700 | $0 | $400 |
| **Total Cost** | **$7,415** | **$624** | **$1,360** |

4. Plan A savings: $6,791; Plan B savings: $6,055
5. $350 per month x 12 months = $4,200
6. Plan A: $1,320; Plan B: $900
7. Plan A would have provided more benefit to this employee. The employee's cost of insurance for Plan A ($1,320) plus his co-pays and deductibles ($624) totals $1,944. The employee's cost of insurance for Plan B ($900) plus co-pays and deductibles ($1,360) totals $2,260. The employee would have saved an additional $316 using Plan A.
8. Plan B would be most beneficial to those who incur few medical costs because the cost of insurance deducted from his pay-check is lower by $420. Although the co-pays and deductibles for Plan B are higher, they may not equal the $420 difference.
9. Yes. Students should realize the necessity and value of medical insurance. They should draw this conclusion based on the calcula-tions they made in question 4. If a more serious injury occurred, their cost without insurance could be substantially higher.